MY JOURNEY FROM HOMELESS TO ABUNDANCE

Creating the Life You Want: Owning Your Own Greatness

STEVE HARDING

BALBOA.
PRESS

A DIVISION OF HAY HOUSE

Balboa Press books may be ordered through booksellers or by contacting:

Balboa Press
A Division of Hay House
1663 Liberty Drive
Bloomington, IN 47403
www.balboapress.com
1 (877) 407-4847

Because of the dynamic nature of the Internet, any web addresses or
links contained in this book may have changed since publication and
may no longer be valid. The views expressed in this work are solely those
of the author and do not necessarily reflect the views of the publisher,
and the publisher hereby disclaims any responsibility for them.

The author of this book does not dispense medical advice or prescribe the use
of any technique as a form of treatment for physical, emotional, or medical
problems without the advice of a physician, either directly or indirectly. The
intent of the author is only to offer information of a general nature to help
you in your quest for emotional and spiritual well-being. In the event you use
any of the information in this book for yourself, which is your constitutional
right, the author and the publisher assume no responsibility for your actions.

Any people depicted in stock imagery provided by Getty Images are
models, and such images are being used for illustrative purposes only.
Certain stock imagery © Getty Images.

Print information available on the last page.

ISBN: 978-1-9822-3425-6 (sc)
ISBN: 978-1-9822-3426-3 (e)

Balboa Press rev. date 09/10/2019

DEDICATION

For

Sherry Hartley

cofounder of Compass Rose

For her dedication, patience, wisdom and love, without which I could never have taken this wonderful and amazing journey!

Table of Contents

Introduction

My "Journey" began in early January of 2011 when I, after losing my wealth over the last 3 years, found myself homeless. I lived in an abandoned house that was in the repossession process, with no running water and most of the time without electricity. I was using the local grocery store as my "facilities" and existing on about 500 calories a day. During the 5 months I was in this situation I lost over 40 pounds.

Even though the physical aspect of being homeless was very uncomfortable it was not the worst part. The worst part was that I woke up each morning with no hope – no way in which I could see how my situation was going to change. I was angry, frustrated, frightened and very much alone with no way out.

Let me share with you a little about my life and what brought me to this place. I believe that will help you see the true shock I felt at being in this position.

I grew up in an upper middle class family in the Northwest. My Dad owned his own business and we were a "well to do" family although I did not realize it while I was growing up. I graduated from college and joined the Navy. I was a Naval Aviator and over the period of my time as a pilot in Vietnam and as a flight instructor I made over 300 carrier landings.

Upon leaving the Service I went into the corporate world and had a very successful career ending up owning my own consulting business that generated a very substantial income during the 15 years I operated it. In 2007 I retired with great expectations for my future. It was at this time that I started down the path that was to lead me to homelessness. In 2006 and 2007 I invested the retirement funds I had accumulated into my home and several rental properties. The real estate market crashed and I lost everything. I managed to survive for the next three years doing jobs I could find but in January of 2011 there I was with no money and in a house with no water or electricity. I was in total disbelief!

However, it was out of this devastating position that I would learn the power of "Owning My Own Greatness" and thereby create the life of peace, joy and abundance I now live. It was out of this situation that this book was born. I hope it is one that will help anyone who has a situation in their life that makes them unhappy decide what they want, ask for it and then experience it – exactly as they do want.

You certainly do not have to be homeless to use the power of your own greatness to change your life. If it is a financial situation, career change, unsatisfying relationship or just a general lack of joy, peace and fun in your life that you want to see differently or perhaps all is well but you are looking for a different direction or "what is next". Understanding the power of "who you really are" can help you along the way. It will give you the tools to command and receive whatever you desire.

During my transformation from being homeless to being abundant I was able to identify and put into practice a "process" that is totally teachable, repeatable and works every time to create whatever you want in your life. The steps in this "process" are simple and begin with "baby steps" to help you build your manifestation muscles.

You learn how to take complete responsibility for your life which gives you the freedom and power to create. You are no longer held back by the actions of others. You will become "completely independent of the good and bad opinion of others". Literally "fearless in the face of any challenge"! This step alone can totally transform your life.

Then by using ancient wisdom and current scientific knowledge you learn why this process works. It is not based on luck or chance but on proven Universal laws. The basis for our ability to change our lives is revealed to us in the theory of Quantum Physics. You will learn to put these laws to work for you. They are already working in your life every day. Why not use them to your advantage?

One of the first things I did in my transformation was to understand the power and importance of gratitude. I developed rituals which I share in the book on how to feel this gratitude and then to be able to use that gratitude to bring more things into my life for which to be grateful. This is still a daily practice for me, and it still works.

The book shares how to bring clarity to what you want to change in your life and then how to decide what you want to change it to; a practice most of us spend no time doing. We tend to live our lives on the "hamster wheel" in a totally reactive mentality and then blame "them" for our situation. Owning your own greatness will break you out of that spiral and bring you into control of what is happening and then show you how to direct it to where you want to go.

Once you know what you really want how you ask for it makes all the difference on whether you receive. The book shows how the ancient Shamans brought rain when they asked for it; why they were successful. A practice you will learn to put into effect to bring whatever you ask for into your life.

After you ask there are things you must do in order to allow what you have asked for to come into your life. Most of us actually drive the things we want away from us by our thoughts and actions and wonder why our lives do not change. There are practices and exercises described that will allow your wishes to flow to you with ease.

When the process begins to work in your life your confidence in it will grow. When I was ready to move out of my no water, no electricity house to a condominium with a waterfront view I signed a contract to move in 45 days and my income was $407.38 a month! But when the 45 days had passed, I not only had the rent money but also enough money to pay all my living expenses and buy all the food I needed!

The process described in "My Journey" is not the only path to creating the life you want but my hope is that it will resonate with some people and guide them to their dreams. I wrote this book because I wanted to share what I have learned so others may benefit and then perhaps share what they receive with even more people.

Thank you.

Chapter 1

Taking Responsibility
The Key to Personal Freedom

"Steve, why did you choose to be homeless?" That was the toughest question I have ever had to ask myself! But it had to be asked because until I took total responsibility for being where I was right now in my life there was nothing I could do to change it in the future.

During the first two months I was in the homeless situation I was really into the "blame game". I was angry, frustrated, confused and afraid. This was directed at everyone I had met over the past year. All the ones who had let me down, lied to me, did not keep their word and just plain cheated me - from my point of view. I put the responsibility on them all and felt ripped off! How could they do this? I am a good person, never hurt anyone; yet here I was. There is no way I deserved this!

But finally, I realized and had to admit the truth. I was here as a result of the choices I had made over the last few years. I was the one "at fault" for my situation. It was not an easy pill to swallow but it had to be done. Why?

Because if I blamed others for my situation I was giving them responsibility for my life and if "they" had the power to put me here how was I ever going to be able to gain control and get out of this mess. But if I took the position that I was here because of my reactions to events and decisions I had made in my past then all I had to do was make different decisions and my life could change into whatever my new decisions created. It was truly all up to me.

Now I will tell you again that this was not an easy admission to accept. I think we all want to look at outside events as the cause of our present situations, especially if they are not pleasant. But the key here is that in order to consciously create our lives we must become aware of and accept responsibility for our actions. Only then can we expect to create our life as we want it to be.

I will also tell you that once I accepted the fact that I was responsible for my life I felt a sense of power and freedom that is difficult to describe. Suddenly I had control over how my life turned out. I could be the one who made conscious choices so I knew where I was headed. Never again would I have to say "I would never choose this for myself" because now I was going to make the choices I wanted consciously. If I made a choice that did not turn out the way I wanted I could make a different choice. Wow, that was powerful, and I was thrilled.

I can write this book and share my experience with you today because I took responsibility for being homeless. I know that I am the Captain of my ship.

The other thing I had to understand was that I was in the perfect place to begin my new journey. All the choices I had made that led me to the homeless situation were the ones I needed to make in order to move forward from this point. There could be no blame, regrets or self punishment for where I was right now. This was the exact place to be for me to start anew.

This is so important because it was the first step towards knowing that I am whole, perfect and complete just the way I am. We all are the amazing person we need to be in order to create our future exactly the way we want it. Begin right now to see how amazing you are, how powerful you are. Begin right now to "own your own greatness"! This is the foundation you must work from to become the person you want to be. Love yourself just the way you are right now!

Let's get started. How do we begin this process of becoming aware and taking responsibility for our actions?

Jack Canfield, coauthor of "Chicken Soup for the Soul" and a great teacher of success puts it the clearest way I have come across. He says there is a formula that we need to understand when making choices in our lives. That formula is:

$$E + R = O$$

In this formula E means the event that has occurred, R means our reaction to that event and O means the outcome of the event caused by our reaction to it.

Now the event can be anything that happens to us, from the simple missing of a turn while driving to the death of a loved one. If you begin to think of your life as a series of events the formula will become clear.

However, we spend very little time during our day conscious of what is occurring in the moment. We live our life pretty much asleep to the present. We wake up in the morning, jump on the hamster wheel and our days seem to just zip by as a series of things that just "happen to us". We have become unconscious bundles of reactions without ever considering what those reactions will create.

I call this the "Pepsi syndrome" meaning when something happens – a "Pepsi" button is pushed in our life then a Pepsi is coming out – automatically.

Most of us have experienced the situation where our Mother, Brother, Sister, Husband, wife or a perfect stranger has said something to us; pushed a Pepsi button, and we just react. Many times this reaction results in anger or frustration. It is an automatic reflex; they just pushed our button and it is their fault, right?

Let's look at that from the viewpoint of our equation. The event, whatever was said, created a reaction in us and this resulted in an outcome – perhaps not pleasant. We now have a situation to deal with and we probably do not even associate our reaction with the outcome – it was totally unconscious.

As I looked back over my life for the year prior to my being homeless I could see this scenario played out many times. An event occurred and I would react unconsciously not considering the outcome and eventually I found myself homeless. I was responsible for the ultimate outcome through these individual choices. They were subconscious; but they were choices. I could have chosen a different reaction resulting in a different outcome.

What is the key here? We must look at our lives consciously, in the present, as a series of events requiring choices which result in outcomes. Only if we are "awake" can we pick the outcome that suits us and then choose a reaction that moves us toward our chosen outcome.

For example, I have a dear friend who is very conscious of her weight, so she eats healthy foods and exercises regularly – she works at it; and is very fit. My friend loves her Mother, but they have one continuing point of contention. Whenever visiting my friend her Mom always comments on the fact that my friend is too thin and should eat more (the event). My friend, because of the effort she puts into maintaining her weight, goes nuts when she hears this (the reaction). It always ends up in a confrontation and uncomfortable situation, not a loving one (the outcome). Going back to my earlier thought, my friend has a "Pepsi button" reaction to her Mom's comment.

Let's look at this situation in the context of our equation. First, Mom grew up in the depression, food was scarce, and people were undernourished in her home. She sees thin as a sign of not enough to eat, something she certainly does not want for her daughter. My friend, who works hard at her appearance and is constantly exposed to the social hypnosis of "thin equates to beauty" hears her Mom as negating her efforts and criticizing her. Both are coming from an unconscious perspective.

Now Mom is probably not going to overcome living in the depression. However, if my friend, who loves her Mom and cherishes their relationship, can get conscious to the situation, remember that the "Pepsi button" she has used in the past does not work and see that she has a choice in how she reacts and could, by making a different choice, completely change the outcome both in the present situation and for the entire visit.

What if, when Mom commented on her build, my friend smiled, gave her Mom a hug and said, "Mom I know you are concerned about me but I can assure you that I am perfectly healthy and getting plenty to eat; thank you for loving me"? See how the Outcome in our equation would be different?

What we are talking about is simple but not easy. Living in the moment and being conscious of our actions is radically different than how we normally live. But the reward for present moment awareness is a life we choose instead of one that just "happens" to us. It is part of the first step to creating the life we want!

Now, there are three more actions we can take in order to accept responsibility for the outcomes we experience and have true freedom in our lives.

First, we must accept the present situation as perfect. Everything right now is just the way it should be. "What, are you nuts – I am homeless – how can that be perfect?" That was the question I asked when I first realized this requirement for freedom. But let's go back to our equation. Because of choices I have made in the past; here I am. Now I do not have to like the results of the choices I have made but I do have to accept the results as they are now.

Then I can reach the following conclusion. The way things are now is exactly where I need to be in order to change them. The perfect place to begin to change is from where you are right now. Think about it. You do not have to move somewhere else to begin to make different choices. You can start from right here. Furthermore, the way things are right now is just the way they are right now; they do not have to remain this way in the future because you have the power to change them, starting now! From this perfect place you can begin to create the results you consciously choose. That knowledge is freedom. So right now, stop using energy wishing things were different!

The second thing you must do at this point is to wake up. You must realize that you have been asleep while making past choices previously and become aware of future choices from now on. This requires some effort because it is not the way we are used to operating. We have been operating pretty much like the dogs in Pavlov's experiment. Every time Pavlov fed his dogs, he rang a bell. Soon every time he rang the bell the dogs would begin to salivate. We, most of the time, have become like the dogs. Ring a bell and we begin to salivate; an unconscious reaction to an outside event.

What I did to help me wake up was to become (takes practice) aware of when my breathing changed. When I felt my breathing rate change I became aware of what emotions I was feeling. In other words, when some event occurred, I just became aware of whether I felt good or bad. I call this a 'tummy check". If I felt good I would make the choice I was considering but if I felt bad I would stop and consider what the outcome of the choice I was considering would bring about. Is this the outcome I want? If not then I could consciously look at different outcomes, choose the one I wanted and respond to the event in a way that would result in the preferred outcome. This is simply making conscious choices and having your life look like you want. Right now, begin to wake up and choose conscious reactions.

The third and final thing that will result in freedom and the life you desire is to adopt the attitude of "defenselessness". This means stop making excuses for how your life is now. It is just how it is, and you are responsible for it so just thank goodness that we can move on from here. It will shortly be in the past. Again, do not spend your energy feeling bad about things or wishing they were different. There is nothing to gain by using energy to defend your position. There is real peace in this response. Remember, you are whole, perfect and complete just the way you are – right now.

What I have described here are the first things I did in order to begin moving out of poverty and homelessness. They were the first steps toward a life of abundance, peace and joy. You do not have to be homeless to make these changes in your life. Whatever you would like to be different you can change. Start by taking responsibility for and accepting how it is now. Begin making conscious choices that result in the outcomes you desire and do not beat yourself up about your present situation.

We are on our way!

Chapter 2

Why Does This All Work?
Spirituality Meets Science

Now that I had taken responsibility for my homeless situation and therefore had the power to create the life I wanted it was time to move on to creating that life. But what was the next step?

Before I go into that I want to explore with you how things are created in this physical world in which we exist. Let's do this by looking at two points of view – the Spiritual view and the scientific view. It is very interesting how these two points of view have merged together over the course of time. Let's look.

I once read a quote by the late author and teacher Wayne Dyer. It went like this; "Years ago if you would have asked a scientist "do you believe in God?" they would have said "of course not, I am a scientist". But if you were to ask a scientist today that same question they would answer "of course I do, I am a scientist!" This quote sums up the change in thinking based on the theory of quantum physics.

As long as I have been consciously traveling down my Spiritual path, I have heard the phrase "we are all connected". But truthfully, I never really thought about what that meant or why it was important. I guess if I visualized it at all I saw it as all humanity being connected by something that looked like a huge spider web and that it was important because I could feel the pain or joy of others all over the planet.

Wow, I could not have been more wrong! "We are all connected", sometimes called the "Unity principle", is one of the basic Laws upon which the entire Universe operates. It is the foundation of our ability to create and the fact that we are manifesting everything that happens in our life! Let's look at it in more depth.

As with all Universal Laws the concept of Unity is not new. One of the earliest references to it was found in the Dead Sea Scrolls written around 400 BC. These scrolls stated, "as above, so below, as within so without, as the universe, so the soul". Deepak Chopra, in his book "The Seven Spiritual Laws of Success" quotes ancient Vedic seers as exclaiming "I am that, you are that, all this is that and that's all there is!" Jesus shared "I and the Father are one!" These statements indicate that early on there was a knowing by some that everything is made of the same stuff.

Now let's move to the late 1800's and early 1900's with names like Max Planck, Albert Einstein, and Werner Heisenberg who, among others, developed the science known as Quantum Mechanics. In terms I can grasp Quantum Mechanics says that everything in the Universe is really made up of energy; nothing is solid. It is all sort of a "Quantum Soup" out there, including us by the way. For those of us who look for "scientific evidence" of the idea that we are all connected and are creating our lives with our thoughts this should help.

If we look at all we have discussed from the point of view that we are all made up of this energy and there are no edges or well defined lines in this energy then we, that is our physical bodies, are really a sort of wiggle, fluctuation or whirlpool in this larger sea of quantum soup. This energy makes up the entire universe so all of "that" is our extended body. We are not just connected to everything we ARE everything. Our physical bodies, along with everything we perceive to be solid, are just expressions of this energy. Much like a wave is simply an expression of the entire ocean.

There are a couple of interesting characteristics about this "quantum soup". First, it is a flowing vibrating energy, again, nothing solid. So, what the human nervous system does, using our five senses, is freeze this soup into solid particles that we then perceive as our solid world – our reality, if you will, which includes our physical bodies.

Secondly, our nervous system freezes this energy into solid particles that relate to what we expect to see based on our history of observation and experience. This is important; we see what we "expect" to see. To quote the movie "What the Bleep Do We Know", the Mayan Indians could not "see" the Spanish ships approaching on the water because they had no experience with which to compare that particular vibration of energy. Remember, the eyes do not see, the brain sees by taking in the image that the eyes send it and comparing those images to what it has "seen" before. So, if our brain has not "seen" that particular image before it will not register. It is interesting that their "Shamans" or Spiritual leaders were the first to see the ships.

Another point to support this theory is that no one sees any object or event the same. When you ask five people to describe something you will get five different interpretations all based on the "expectations" or history of those individuals relating to that object.

So, assuming Einstein and his fellow scientists are correct, in fact we freeze our extended bodies into what we expect it to look like. It could be said that our expectations are a result of our thoughts. A logical conclusion could then be reached that our thoughts, using our five senses, determine how we freeze the quantum soup into what we see as our daily life. How important does that make our thoughts? How critical does it become to pay attention to what we think?

Scientists who study this sort of thing say we have between 50,000 and 60,000 thoughts a day. The interesting thing is that 90% of the thoughts we have today are the same thoughts we had yesterday and will have tomorrow. If you focus on this for a moment you will see the truth in that statement. We have really turned ourselves into bundles of subconscious reactions to our outside stimulus. This, for lack of a better word, non-thinking approach to our every day existence could result in our life seeming to repeat itself over and over in cycles. Does that sound familiar to anyone?

The key to breaking these cycles, since our thoughts are responsible for freezing the energy into reality, is to understand that each thought we have generates a choice. Instead of just continuing on auto pilot we can become present to the choices available and select the one that will "freeze" into the reality we want.

For example, remember my friend whose Mother pushed her "anger" button? Instead of choosing a reaction that froze into stress and confrontation she could have stopped for a second and consciously chose to be loving and compassionate toward her Mother and the "frozen" reality would have reflected peace and harmony.

This being aware and choosing consciously is a concept that is weak in most of us. Therefore, the Unity principle is very important in the living of our life. We are not just connected; we are all made from the same thing that the entire Universe is made of and through our thoughts we freeze this Quantum soup into what becomes our reality – our physical life.

A scientific study conducted by the Weismann Institute in 1998 concluded that in the Quantum world the observer in an experiment affects the outcome. Using what we have learned from both science and spiritual thinkers if we became conscious observers of our thoughts, we could powerfully affect the outcome of this experiment we call our life. Our conscious (or unconscious) thoughts literally become the things we see in our life.

Chapter 3

Creating by Choosing - Consciously

We now have an understanding, both scientific and spiritual, of how through our thoughts we create the reality we see around us. This knowledge allows us to move into the next phase of creating the life we desire – choosing. There are two parts to this phase; first, getting present to our thoughts. Second, visualizing what we want our lives to look like.

The first step is perhaps the most difficult for the simple reason we have never learned how or spent any time practicing being present to our thoughts. As humans most of our thoughts either regret the past or fear the future. Our thoughts are spent looking back at what has already occurred and how it is affecting us now or looking forward to what might happen in the future and how we can deal with it. This creates a life that appears totally reactionary. It seems as if our life is flowing by us much like a movie on a screen and we are simply reacting to what we see in the way that best minimizes our regrets or avoids our fears.

However, we now know that the movie is actually being created by our thoughts so it is possible, by becoming aware of our thoughts in the present and then directing them toward our desires, we can "get out in front of the movie" and consciously create the events on the screen. Then using on the E + R = O equation we can choose reactions to those events that will result in the life we want. We can now become consciously responsible for the life we are living. How powerful is that!?

It is very powerful! But what is next?

The key word in the above sentence is "consciously". We spend very little time being conscious of our thoughts; they just seem to fly past us. Many of us just get out of our bed and jump on the "hamster wheel", run all day long and at night fall into bed wondering what it is all about.

The most important lesson we can learn in creating the life we desire is to GET PRESENT TO THIS MOMENT! This means being aware of our thoughts right now. As Ram Dass states "Be Here Now"! In order to do this, we must STOP our thoughts and focus on them. Like many of the lessons in this book this is like going to the gym and building a muscle that we have not used in the past. The way to begin this is to create "triggers" that alert you to get present. Choose some common activities that you do during the day and use them to remind you to be present to your thoughts at that moment.

One exercise I do to accomplish this is when I open the door to walk out of my house, I take a moment and focus on the soles of my feet. Bring your awareness to the bottom of your feet. Just feel them, how they fit into your shoes, the surface they are resting on. Can you feel the blood running through them? Close your eyes if that helps.

Another time I do this focus exercise is when I sit down in my car. Before driving away, I close my eyes and project a safe and comfortable result for the trip I am about to take.

How about whenever you climb a set of stairs? Stop your thoughts and get present to what you want the next few minutes to look like. If you practice these exercises and create more of them that work for you the "get present" muscle will become stronger and over time it will be easier for you to operate in the "now".

Notice how your thoughts slow down during these moments; that they are focused, and you are aware of exactly what they are. This is the state of awareness you must be in to create. You must be consciously aware of your thoughts in order to direct them. It is in the "now" that your future is born. I cannot emphasize enough how important this exercise is. If you will do this, you can create your life by directing your thoughts in this moment toward what you desire.

The second or visualizing part of choosing our life seems like it would be easy does it not? However, this presents a problem very similar to the one we just discussed – getting present to our thoughts. Why? Because just as we spend virtually no time being present to our thoughts in this moment, we spend even less time consciously focusing on what we want our lives to look like. Again, we spend most of our time "on the hamster wheel" reacting to the situations we encounter. We are "too busy" to spend time quietly and clearly picturing our ideal life. An analogy would be that if we unconsciously go back and forth between green and blue, we should not be surprised if yellow shows up.

Think back over the last few days. How many times did you consciously think about what you wanted your life to look like? This does not mean how much time you spent thinking that you were not happy with your life; although even that would be a step up for most of us. I am talking about quietly, consciously focusing on how you want your day to look. If you can say "five minutes" you are way ahead of most of humanity.

When we are going on a vacation or trip do we not plan it? Make hotel reservations, pack according to the weather we will encounter, use a map to find the route? Think in advance how we want it to turn out? Furthermore, the planning is a lot of fun and a very enjoyable part of the vacation. But most of us spend very little time on vacation. Doesn't it make sense to put the same planning and advance thinking into how we are going to spend most of our life; into how we want our non vacation time to turn out?

When I was in school, especially grade school, I would often get into trouble for "daydreaming". Letting my mind wander into the future and what fun things I had planned. Daydreaming included visualizing in my mind the coming events and how they would feel when I finally got out of school and experienced them. Daydreaming can be one of the most powerful tools we have for creating our future. Think about it. When we are daydreaming we are both conscious of our thoughts in this moment and picturing and feeling what we want our future to look like.

There are two key points here. First, we are consciously, in the moment, taking time to focus on what we want our future to look like. That is the vehicle for creating our future – our thoughts in this moment become our future things.

Second and perhaps even more importantly as we are in the daydream, we are feeling the emotions that this life we are thinking about will give us. The joy, the peace and the fun we will be having when we are experiencing this life. Emotions are the fuel that drives the vehicle. The more powerful the emotions we feel the faster the Universe will line up the necessary details to give us the life we desire.

We are introducing a new concept here that will become very critical in our next phase of creating the life we desire – asking for what we want. While you are experiencing the emotions of your "daydream" begin to feel as if what you desire is already in your life. Feel as if you were living the reality of it right now. This is the foundation for the asking phase of creation.

Take some time, even if it is only five minutes a day at first, and daydream about your life and how you want it to be. Allow yourself to have fun doing this. Enjoy it to the maximum. If you do this, you will find that you will naturally make more time available to spend picturing and enjoying the future you are creating.

Finally, be alert to the present so that when the things you are daydreaming about start showing up in your life – and they will – you are aware of the progress and your time spent creating the future will be even more effective and fun.

Get present to your thoughts, choose, then create and enjoy your life every day!

Chapter 4

Gratitude and Asking; the Connection

The house I was staying in during my homeless period was in the process of repossession. It was torn up inside and the owner, a long time friend who visited occasionally, kept all the doors inside locked except for the one to my bedroom. My bedroom had a chair, a TV, which was difficult to watch since I had no electricity, and an air mattress bed which leaked so that I had to awaken several times during the night and blow it up. All in all, it was not a pleasant existence.

However, as I began to take responsibility for my situation, and I spent time becoming aware of that responsibility and aware of my thoughts regarding my situation I realized that I had the power to change my circumstances. But what did I want my life to look like?

This is when I started to understand that how I asked for more pleasant life circumstances made the difference in how quickly I received them. Here is how that understanding manifested.

I decided that I wanted to move back into a two bedroom two bath condominium that looked out over the water! That was my goal. So, each morning as I woke up, usually even before I opened my eyes, I imagined that someday I would wake up in my new condo. However, when I did open my eyes, I realized I was in a torn up house with no electricity, no running water and I had no money. The whole imagining exercise seemed not only impossible but ridiculous. I felt even more depressed than before I did the exercise.

What I was missing was the fact that all our thoughts have what Neal Donald Walsch described in his wonderful book "Conversations With God, Book 1" a "sponsoring thought". The "sponsoring thought" is the thought that lies below the surface thought we are having at that moment. We must "peel the onion" to a deeper level in order to become aware of what the sponsoring thought is. The sponsoring thought represents the true vibration of the thought and is what the Universe recognizes and uses to create. Now when we peel it down to the lowest level of thought there are only two. Our base sponsoring thoughts come from either "fear" or "love". All our thoughts are generated from one of these two places. In other words, our thoughts can either make us feel bad or make us feel good.

Let me give you a couple of personal examples. When I think "I want to win the lottery" the next thought is usually something like "right, what are the odds", then "I have basically zero chance", finally, "I will be in this financial situation forever". The basis for this series of thoughts or the "sponsoring" thought is fear so the Universe creates based on my fear of lack and I continued to experience it.

Another example is "I want to live in a two bedroom two bath condo on the water". That was so far away from what I believed was possible that it was "sponsored" by the fear of never being able to change my situation. It was just too big of a leap to believe in.

It is extremely important to understand that currently I was not consciously aware of the concept of "sponsoring thoughts". I had not read Mr. Walsch's book. What is so important about this is that I now know that I am, as we all are, divinely guided toward a joyful and peaceful life. The only thing required is to take responsibility for our situation and quietly listen for the guidance that will come. We must have the courage or "faith the size of a mustard seed" to act on the guidance we receive. That is the whole foundation upon which the process described in this book is built. The guidance I had is available to each of us, but we must open our hearts to it. We live in a friendly and loving Universe.

However, even though I did not understand why what I was trying to do was so powerful, I refused to give up on the idea that there was a way to create something different in my life. Just the knowing in my heart that I was the power behind my life gave me the strength to continue searching for a way out. I was really starting to believe in myself and it was a wonderful feeling!

What came to me is that perhaps I should start smaller in my intentions. I knew the way was there but maybe I was looking too far too fast. I decided that the place to begin was to find something that was already in my life, something I could see right now, and be thankful that I already had it. At the time I had this insight I did not realize that it was the key to manifesting anything I wanted in my life!

This is the connection between "the sponsoring" thoughts we have and the Quantum energy that makes up everything. The most important component for manifesting anything is not to ask for it in supplication but to feel the love, gratitude and appreciation as if what we want already exists in our life!

When the American Indian shamans were asked to create rain, they did not ask the Gods for rain. Instead they would focus on the gratitude for the rain as if it already existed. They would feel the rain on their clothes, feel the mud under their moccasins, see the crops that were growing because of the rain and generate the powerful energy of gratitude to the Gods for that rain. The strong vibration of gratitude for the rain was the power that created the rain.

The most powerful vibration in the Universe is love. It is followed closely by gratitude. These vibrations are what the Universe, God or Source – you pick the word that works for you – responds to. We live in a friendly Universe that wants to give us what we desire; all the time. We need to communicate with this Universe in a language it understands and responds to. Everything in the Universe has a vibrational frequency. The things that make us feel good vibrate at a higher frequency than the things that make us feel bad. When we feel grateful for the things we want and appreciate having them in our life we raise the frequency of our thoughts to match the vibration frequency of the things we want, and they are attracted into our lives. There is an amazing book by Abraham Hicks called "Ask and It is Given" that explains this concept simply and in a way we can really understand. I highly recommend it.

What I decided to do in my search for a way out of homelessness was to pick two things I already had in my life and feel a powerful sense of gratitude for them. I picked the fact that I had a roof over my head. I was not on the streets or in a shelter. And I had my health.

After choosing those two things I began a ritual that I have done virtually every day of my life since that morning. I call it my "gratitude exercise".

Immediately after waking up I begin to breathe deeply. I cross my arms over my chest with my eyes closed. I do these things because the physical motions help me create the mind set necessary to do the exercise. You can pick anything that settles your thoughts.

I then begin to feel gratitude for whatever I wanted or had as if it were the very blood flowing through my veins. I opened my heart and let the grateful feelings consume my entire body. It was almost as if my physical being disappeared and I became only the feeling of gratitude and thankfulness. I repeated in my thoughts "thank you, thank you, thank you".

There is no time frame for this. I only do it for as long as I can remain in this state of gratitude comfortably. Then, while continuing to breathe deeply, I uncross my arms and begin to return to my waking state. The feeling of peace and love remains for a few minutes then I am ready to start my day. I do this every morning and then several times during the day I will focus on feelings of gratitude and repeat the words "thank you" either aloud or in my thoughts.

After I began doing this exercise in the mornings nothing in my physical world changed but soon, I began to feel lighter, happier and I started smiling more often and then even laughing occasionally. Then one day the friend who owned the house visited and forgot to lock the door to another bedroom. I went into this bedroom and there was a beautiful bed with clean sheets, a window that the sun was shining through, and light was everywhere. I immediately moved into this bedroom and added it to my gratitude list. Strangely, my friend never came to the house again.

As I continued this exercise small things that increased my comfort began showing up in my life. As I felt stronger in my belief in the power of gratitude, I began putting things into my exercise that were not already in my life and they would somehow to show up. For example, I found the money to pay for gas so I could begin to attend the Unity church in St. Petersburg, and I would stay for both services. What a great opportunity to express my gratitude.

Every Sunday on my way to and from Church I would pass a condominium complex that was on the water. One day I decided to stop and check in with the real estate office that handled that complex. I asked the agent if she knew of any condos for rent there. We looked on her computer and found one that I loved. I asked her how much the rent was. At that time my income was $407.38 a month from a retirement fund that I had recently discovered I had earned – more grist for the gratitude exercise!

When the agent told me how much the rent was, I asked to look at a contract and signed it agreeing to move in 45 days later. Wow, I was trusting in my ability to create! Then every Sunday on my way home I would stop at the complex, sit outside the one that I had rented and powerfully feel the gratitude in my body for being able to live in that condo. I would picture myself walking around in it, cooking in the kitchen and waking up in the bed.

About three weeks after I began the Sunday ritual of stopping at the condo I got a phone call from a friend I had not heard from in over a year. When he asked me how I was doing I laughingly explained my situation to him. He reminded me of an income opportunity that he had shared with me a long time ago and I had ignored. I revisited this opportunity and within a week had created the income necessary for me not only to move into the condo but pay all my expenses and buy food! I moved into that two bedroom two bath condo on the water on the day I had agreed to in the contract and I live on the water today.

I now, for obvious reasons, believe totally in the idea that whatever we desire to have in our lives we do not ask for it from a position of not having it but from the feeling of complete and total gratitude for already having it in our lives. Love and gratitude are powerful forces that the Universe hears and responds to.

If you think about this a little more deeply it makes perfect sense. When we go to the Universe from the position of "wanting" something we are putting out the vibration of lack or not having it but wanting it. The wanting comes from the sponsoring thought of fear and so the wanting is what we continue to get. But when we come from the vibration of already having it and being grateful the Universe responds by bringing it into our reality. Love and gratitude must be our "sponsoring thought".

An attitude of gratitude is the connection between our desires and the manifestation of them into our life.

Chapter 5

What Do I Do Next - No Action Required, Just Peace

We have now taken responsibility for our own life, we accept things as perfect just the way they are, we have become aware of our thoughts, consciously decided what we want and felt the gratitude of having what we wanted with the sponsoring thought of love. What is the next step?

Many of the steps we have discussed so far may seem difficult because they require thinking in a different way than we have been trained by the world we normally operate in to think. The next, and last, step is no different.

The final step in creating our desired life is to do nothing; to just become quiet and still during periods throughout the day. It is time to let go and "let the Universe handle the details". This is a discipline we are not very comfortable with.

For most of my "successful" life I considered myself a "get 'er done" kind of guy, a "rainmaker" if you will. The clichés are many and well known. "If you want it done right do it yourself", just "make it happen", "you can only depend on yourself", "if you want it you must work hard for it", "nothing comes easy" and on and on. This is what we have been taught since we were little. It is the "American way". We believe that if we are not in control and forcing the issue nothing is happening. The problem with this mentality is that it not only severely limits our ability to create but also causes stress, hypertension, worry and sometimes heart attacks. We are constantly pushing against what is so by trying to create life situations as we want them to be. What we have come to believe is that when we desire an outcome it is up to us to figure out how the outcome will be manifested and then create the circumstances necessary for that to happen. It is a lot of hard work.

Let's examine this a little closer.

First, let's look at the difference between the tools we as human beings have to create outcomes and what the Universe or Source has available to it. If we go back to Chapter two and review how the Universe works, we remember the entire Universe is composed of a flowing vibrating and thinking energy. There is an inherent intelligence in this Quantum soup. It is what many refer to as a "field of all possibilities". Another way of saying this is that there are already in existence in this energy field an infinite number of potential ways for an outcome to be manifested.

Now let's look at what we humans have available to us in order to create an outcome. In our physical realm we cannot see all the potential ways something can happen. The only tool we have available to us is our past. Our memory of how things have occurred in the short time we have spent on the planet. So, when we try to figure out how what we desire can be manifested two important things happen.

First, we severely limit ourselves because we are trying to create the future based only upon on our past. Those few things we have experienced up to this point in our lives.

Second, we tend to lock onto what we do know based on our experience therefore blinding ourselves to any other possibilities that might be out there. We do not know what we do not know so our field of operation is very small.

Compare this human method of creating to what the Universe can do. When you put an intention out into the Universe it recognizes the vibration of that intention, which we now know is based on love, and begins to organize an infinite number of circumstances necessary for that intention to be fulfilled. It is not limited by what has happened in the past because in the Universe all possibilities are available. Things will be organized that you in your physical form are not even aware exist. Situations will be created that will allow events to flow so that the opportunity for your intention to become reality will occur with no effort on your part. In fact, by trying to make it happen you interfere and slow the process down by putting thoughts of not having it yet into play. We will say more on this later.

Let me share with you the incident that made this creation process totally clear to me. I was sitting on my deck looking out over the water one day. I was very quiet, peaceful and grateful for my life, the importance of which I will discuss later. In Florida we have a bird called a Cormorant, a fish eating bird. The Cormorant is unique in that the way it catches fish is to paddle along on top of the water and then suddenly dive under the water and swim to catch a fish. It disappears while it is doing this. As I sat there observing this Cormorant as he dove under the water a thought occurred to me. "When the Cormorant was under the water and I could not see it does it still exist?" I then thought "of course it still exists I just cannot see him, but he is swimming around catching fish." I live on a very large bay of water and I can see water for a couple of miles in all directions.

Then the epiphany struck me. There was an entire universe of activity going on under the surface of that bay. I was not able to see it, but it was going on all the time! "Wow", I thought, "this is exactly how the Universe or Source operates. It is never still, and an infinite number of actions are taking place that are not within the limits of my physical awareness but in fact are taking place none the less! Furthermore, it is a friendly Universe that wants me to have everything I desire!" Suddenly the ability of the Universe to correlate an infinite number of possibilities to fulfill my intentions became totally real and alive. It was a quantum shift in my reality.

Now, there are a couple of things that are important for us to understand in this creation process. There is a saying, "you just have to get out of your own way" that used to drive me crazy. How can you get out of your own way? As a matter of fact, how can you be in your own way? I wrestled with this for a long time until I realized that it meant relaxing and letting the natural way of things proceed.

Deepak Chopra, in his amazing book "The Seven Spiritual Laws of Success" addresses the "Law of Detachment". He states in this Law that we must put an intention out into the Universe and then "detach" ourselves from the outcome. This is so powerful because it allows the Universe to work in the field of all possibilities without our interference. We interfere in this process when we constantly wonder when our intention will come to us or how is it going to happen or worst of all focusing on not having it yet. I quote many wise people when I say, "you do not plant a seed and then dig it up every day to see if it is growing".

If we understand and believe in our "Cormorant connection" to the Universe we will trust that things are lining up to give us what we have lovingly asked for. So we can just be joyful and peaceful in our daily lives.

In addition to detaching ourselves from the outcome there is one other thing we need to understand about the creation process of the Universe. You may recall the story of my stopping at the real estate office to look at potential condos for rent. Like many things I have learned and discussed in this book the impact of what I was doing was not clear to me at the time I just followed my "instinct" and did what seemed like a good idea.

Here is what I have come to understand. The Universe correlates circumstances, an infinite number of them, in order to bring our intentions into reality. It is important that we remain detached from the outcome. However, we do have a role to play in the manifestation of our intentions. If I intend to have a new car the chances are that I will not walk out into my garage tomorrow and see a new car sitting there. That is not generally how it works, although truly sometimes it seems to be the case.

The Universe creates by aligning circumstances beyond our knowing but then setting up opportunities by which we can play a role in the manifestation of our desires. The beauty of this is that the Universe will provide the opportunities and then guide us to the action required in order to take advantage of the opportunity. We will be guided to the correct path. There are two important things to know about this.

First, the Universe speaks to us in a whisper. The communication is there but we need to have a quiet mind to hear it. This goes back to being present to our thoughts and quietly listening for the direction. It is easier to do this if we expect it and are looking for it. When I had the epiphany, which shifted my reality, about the Cormorant and the Universe I was in a peaceful, quiet and grateful state of mind so the thought came through loud and clear. We must take time each day to be quiet and listen for the guidance. There are many ways of practicing meditation which are excellent and provide an opportunity to hear the guidance. A quiet mind opens the door to hearing where we should go.

Second, once we have heard the guidance, we must have the faith and courage to take the action. We are not very comfortable acting outside of the "hamster wheel" envelope we operate in most of our days; we are just too busy. However, if you open the "quiet" door just a crack the guidance will come and the action necessary will be apparent. Trust your quiet inner voice and step out into what Deepak Chopra refers to as the "wisdom of uncertainty". The known and comfortable is simply our past repeating itself. There is no chance for growth there so we must step outside the past and go for it. Ask yourself "what would I do if I was not afraid". The rewards are huge.

Finally, let me share something with you that will help in the effort to detach, hear the guidance and take the action. The Universe loves you. After all you are directly connected to this friendly loving Universe so it will never give up on you. If you miss the first message there will be a second and a third and a thousandth if necessary. Just trust and let your mind settle into peacefulness. Love yourself and own your own greatness.

Chapter 6

Why Do This - A Purpose Driven Life

Now we have all the pieces of the process available to us. We can, using the tools we have learned, conceivably bring anything we desire into our lives. Again, I want to emphasize that there is nothing new here. I have taken many things I have learned from people much wiser than I and combined them in a way that has allowed me to create a life of peace, abundance and joy. It is my hope that using this material will help someone else achieve their dreams.

I have had opportunities to share this process with others and have witnessed amazing improvements in their circumstances. That gives me even greater joy. That joy brings me to the point I want to share in the final chapter.

I stated in the very beginning that the real pain of being homeless was not so much the difficult physical circumstances but the more powerful lack of hope; the helpless feeling that there was no way out of my situation. What I have come to understand by learning and applying the steps described here is that the exact opposite is true for me now. The joy and peace I am experiencing does not come from my physical surroundings but from the knowing that I have a connection to something much more powerful than the material things I have been fortunate enough to accumulate. I am now able to experience a direct relationship with Source, the Universe or God. It does not matter what I call it because it just IS, and it brings to me pure peace, joy and hope. Its foundation is love.

I know now that the real purpose for my being in this physical form and learning what I have learned through this process I have described was to remember why I came here in the first place. I came into this physical world from a nonphysical realm to create, generate love and experience joy. It was an exciting expectation and one I knew I could manifest because I am an extension of Source. Every living thing on the planet has a direct connection to the Power that orchestrates the entire Universe. I have come to know this connection as my "universal soul" and the steps I have taken since being homeless were the steps necessary for me to once again see the world from the point of view of that "soul" which is the point of view of love.

We all come into the physical realm with the knowing of what we can do and who we really are but by the time we are around eight years old we have forgotten that knowing because we have developed what we believe is a "survival method". A way we must act to get along in this physical world we have been born into.

Ben Franklin said, "most people die by the age of 25 and wait another 50 years to lie down". What he means is that early on we become "hardwired" into a way of existing and are not able to see any other way of being. We have truly jumped onto the "hamster wheel" and we run there for the rest of our lives. We become addicted to the "Pepsi button" reaction and there we stay.

What I have shared in the early chapters are the steps I took in order to regain the knowing of who I really am. The manifestation of the condos, cars and financial security were just a result of my successful reconnection to Source. One of the most powerful understandings resulting from this reconnection is that I can live totally without fear. I know that everything is in Divine order and "all is well" because I am guided by this connection.

The other morning I had the most amazing epiphany I have had in this entire journey. I realized that if I had $10,000,000 in the bank I would not feel any more peaceful and joyful than I do now. Furthermore, if I knew I was going to die tomorrow I would not feel any less peaceful and joyful than I do now!

If I had a magic wand and could wave it so everyone on the planet would have this feeling I would do it instantly. I do not have that wand so hopefully this book will help someone else reach that conclusion.

Thank you!

Exercises

Daily Practices To Build Your Manifestation Muscles

The purpose of the following exercises is to help you become aware of your thoughts. To help you "wake up" and start to be present to what you are thinking and stop operating from the "auto pilot" mode that we are in most of the time. In order to begin to create our lives purposefully we will need to redirect our thoughts away from the subconscious and guide them toward conscious awareness.

This is just like changing the shape of our bodies by going to the gym. It is most effective if we do it consistently beginning with light weights and then moving to heavier ones as we get stronger. Also, like changing the shape of your body the hardest part is starting to go to the gym.

Start with only five minutes right after you wake up to begin consciously thinking and planning how you want your day to unfold. Picture it in your mind and make it a joyful and peaceful picture. Enjoy this few minutes with the amazing person you are – whole, perfect and complete, right now.

Then run through your mind the list of all the things for which you can be grateful. Let this feeling of warmth and gratitude flow through you like the blood in your veins – really feel it. You will soon notice that your days go better, and your life seems to be lighter and more joyful.

On the following pages I have listed exercises that I did and others that I recommend for each of the five steps in the process described in the "Journey". But if you do nothing else but the five minutes of visualizing and gratitude I have just shared you will see a beautiful and fundamental shift in your life.

TAKING RESPONSIBILITY

1. Sit quietly and review in your mind the events that have occurred in the past 24 hours. It may take some focus to break your day down into separate events. This is a great exercise because our life really comes to us as a series of events and recognizing this is critical to changing the outcome of the events and our lives.

   Select two events/ reactions that did not result in an outcome that made you feel good. Review your thoughts about the event and how they contributed to the outcome. Remember, it is important (although maybe not fun) that you look at the event from the point of view that you alone are responsible for the outcome. Include only yourself in the equation. If you find yourself "blaming" others this is a huge red flag and becoming aware of it is important. You want the credit for how your life works.

   Tomorrow review the last 12 hours in the day, the next day review the last 8 hours, then the last 4 hours, then 2 hours. As you shorten the review time each day you are building the E + R = O muscle until you are looking at the last event and finally the event that is happening right now!

   Extra Credit: Begin a daily diary that breaks the day down into events and use it to help in the review process.

2. This is an exercise I have taken from Deepak Chopra's amazing book "The Spontaneous Fulfillment of Desire". Initially it can be a little uncomfortable because it stretches our comfort level in accepting our own greatness. But that is the point, right?

When you find yourself in front of a mirror stop whatever you are doing and focus your attention on your eyes looking back at you. While looking into your own eyes repeat the following three statements out loud.

1. "I am completely and totally independent of the good and bad opinion of others."

2. "I am above no one. I am below no one."

3. "I am fearless in the face of any challenge."

Feel the power of these statements in your soul and look for the light that shines from your eyes. This is who you really are!

CONSCIOUSLY CHOOSING

1. The first part of this exercise is to get present to our thoughts. Remember that our future is created in the thoughts we are having right now – consciously or unconsciously. We want it to be conscious because it is much more fun that way!

   The key to this is to pick some "triggers"; some activities that when you do them it reminds you to become aware of what you are thinking. Perhaps it's brushing your teeth, taking a shower, pausing after you start your car and focusing before you drive away, climbing stairs or drinking your morning coffee. It does not matter what the trigger is, so pick anything that works for you. The important part is to be consistent, so you begin to build the "get present" muscle.

   Now, when the trigger occurs STOP YOUR THOUGHTS! Become present to what they are! What are you thinking? Hear the voice in your head; what is it saying?

   Once you are present to your thoughts refocus them on what you want the next few minutes of your life to look like. For example, one of my triggers is starting my car. I use that to focus my thoughts on having a safe, comfortable and enjoyable trip. I picture arriving at my destination relaxed and peaceful.

   This may seem difficult at first because the "voice of the hamster wheel" is so powerful in most of us. Just be easy with yourself and concentrate on the exercise. It will become easier and the results are powerful and rewarding.

Extra Credit:

When you get focused on what your thoughts are in the present moment ask yourself this question. "Are the thoughts I am thinking making me happy?" Wow, what an insight!

2. The second part of choosing consciously is a lot of fun. We are going to take a few minutes (to begin with; it will get longer as you practice) and go on a "mind vacation". It is OK to call it daydreaming. Abraham Hicks, in her wonderful book "Ask and It Is Given", calls it going to your "workshop". This should be a time when there are no distractions and you can be relaxed.

During this time pick a small segment of your life and picture it as perfect. I say a small segment because it is good to start small and focused. You will grow into longer and larger segments as your "vacation" muscle grows. But for the start you can picture, for example, getting out of bed. What time would it be? Visualize being rested and relaxed. You would be looking forward to a wonderful day – perhaps that is the next segment. Visualize what perfection would look like. Now, and this is important, FEEL the emotions this perfection would generate. BE alive in this feeling, enjoy it! Begin to expect this to be the way your life is.

There is no right or wrong in this part of the exercise. Just have a lot of fun with it. Gosh, isn't it great to just have some relaxed time just for yourself? BE HAPPY! Do this as many times as it is comfortable each day. You will begin to look forward to it.

Love and Gratitude;
Our Connection to Receiving

1. There are only two sponsoring thoughts – love or fear. Every thought we have has at its core the vibration of either love or fear and that core vibration is what the Universe responds to by attracting things into our life. Therefore, it is very important to be aware of which core vibration we are creating from.

   Once again awareness is the key to consciously creating our life. We must get off the "hamster wheel" and be awake to what we are thinking.

   When you experience a "trigger" moment you have selected in the earlier exercise become aware of what you are thinking. Then go one step further and ask yourself "is what I am thinking making me feel good or bad"? That feeling is the indicator of whether the sponsoring thought is fear or love. This is true 100% of the time! Recognizing the way you feel can then help you redirect your thoughts if necessary. If it feels good keep going. If it feels bad consciously change your thoughts to something that does feel good. For example, you can go to the gratitude exercise below.

2. This is the exercise that started me down the path to abundance. I have done it nearly every morning and throughout each day for over 8 years. I call it my "gratitude exercise".

   When I first wake up in the morning, even before I am fully awake, I cross my arms over my chest. This physical action sets the awareness for the exercise. You can use whatever makes sense to you. With my eyes closed I focus on my breathing and slow it down. Then I focus my thoughts on what I already have in my life that I am grateful for and I feel this gratitude as if it were the blood flowing through my veins; let it powerfully take over your physical body. I let this flow through me for a while and then I shift my thoughts to something I want to bring into my life and feel this same gratitude as if it were already there. I feel the joy, peace and love of already experiencing it in my world. I have a knowing that it is there. This should feel very good so let it out! As I come back from the feeling of gratitude I repeat "thank you" over and over in my mind.

Then throughout the day I bring this feeling of gratitude into my thoughts and say "thank you" again.

Even before anything physical changed in my life this exercise created a lighter more joyful feeling in me. Love and gratitude are the most powerful vibrations in the Universe. Use them to create!

Be Still And Let The Universe Handle It

1. There are two critical themes that are woven throughout this process of taking control of our lives. The first is to become aware. To WAKE UP to our thoughts and what is occurring around us. This is a totally new way of thinking for most of us but is mandatory if we want to consciously participate in our own lives. Many of the exercises and processes described are for building this awareness muscle.

   The second theme is living our lives from a place of peaceful awareness. We must become quiet and let the noise in our minds settle. Stopping the "monkey chatter" that goes on constantly in our head is the key to hearing our inner soul.

   There is no better tool to accomplishing this than meditation.

   I know, I know; you do not have time to meditate! You can barely get done what you need to do in the 24 hours you have, right?

   My friends, please. That is the problem we are trying to solve. Does it feel good to run around all day being at the mercy of outside influences? Is your life out of your control? If you keep doing what you are doing, you will keep getting what you are getting!

   Start by doing the gratitude exercise when you wake up. Then after a week add 5 minutes of quiet breathing to the end of the exercise or start with 3 minutes. Build this muscle slowly but build it. The difference will astound you.

There are many forms of meditation that are available so find one that works for you. As mentioned above simply being aware of your breath works or silently repeating "ho hum" in rhythm with your breathing is good as well. If you truly want to change something in your life this exercise will get you started.

Printed in the United States
By Bookmasters